tunes to play t

GH00833041

Volume Two
Arranged by Kenneth Pont

WOODWIND PACK

Contents

Oxford University Press, Walton Street, Oxford OX2 6DP, England
Oxford University Press, 200 Madison Avenue, New York, NY 10016, USA
Oxford is a trade mark of Oxford University Press
Oxford University Press 1991

Music Department
OXFORD UNIVERSITY PRESS
Oxford and New York

Symphony No. 8 in B minor
(Second movement)

Franz Schubert
(1797-1828)

Printed in Great Britain
OXFORD UNIVERSITY PRESS, MUSIC DEPARTMENT, WALTON STREET, OXFORD OX2 6DP

Tunes to Play Together Volume Two

Arranged by Kenneth Pont

Woodwind

Part One

Bb Instrument

Symphony No. 8 in B minor

(Second movement)

Franz Schubert
(1797-1828)

Printed in Great Britain

OXFORD UNIVERSITY PRESS, MUSIC DEPARTMENT, WALTON STREET, OXFORD OX2 6DP

Rosamunde
(Overture)

Franz Schubert
(1797-1828)

Nutcracker Suite Op. 71a
(Valse des fleurs)

Peter Ilyich Tchaikovsky
(1840-93)

Symphony No. 41 in C (K 551)
(Trio)

Wolfgang Amadeus Mozart
(1756-91)

Violin Concerto in E minor Op. 64
(Third movement)

Felix Mendelssohn-Bartholdy
(1809-47)

Tunes to Play Together Volume Two

Arranged by Kenneth Pont

Woodwind

Part Three

B♭ Instrument

Symphony No. 8 in B minor
(Second movement)

Franz Schubert
(1797-1828)

Rosamunde
(Overture)

Franz Schubert
(1797-1828)

Nutcracker Suite Op. 71a

(Valse des fleurs)

Peter Ilyich Tchaikovsky
(1840-93)

Symphony No. 41 in C (K 551)

(Trio)

Wolfgang Amadeus Mozart
(1756-91)

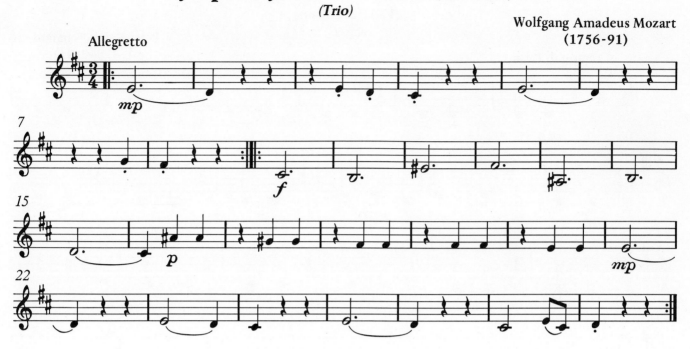

Violin Concerto in E minor Op. 64

(Third movement)

Felix Mendelssohn-Bartholdy
(1809-47)

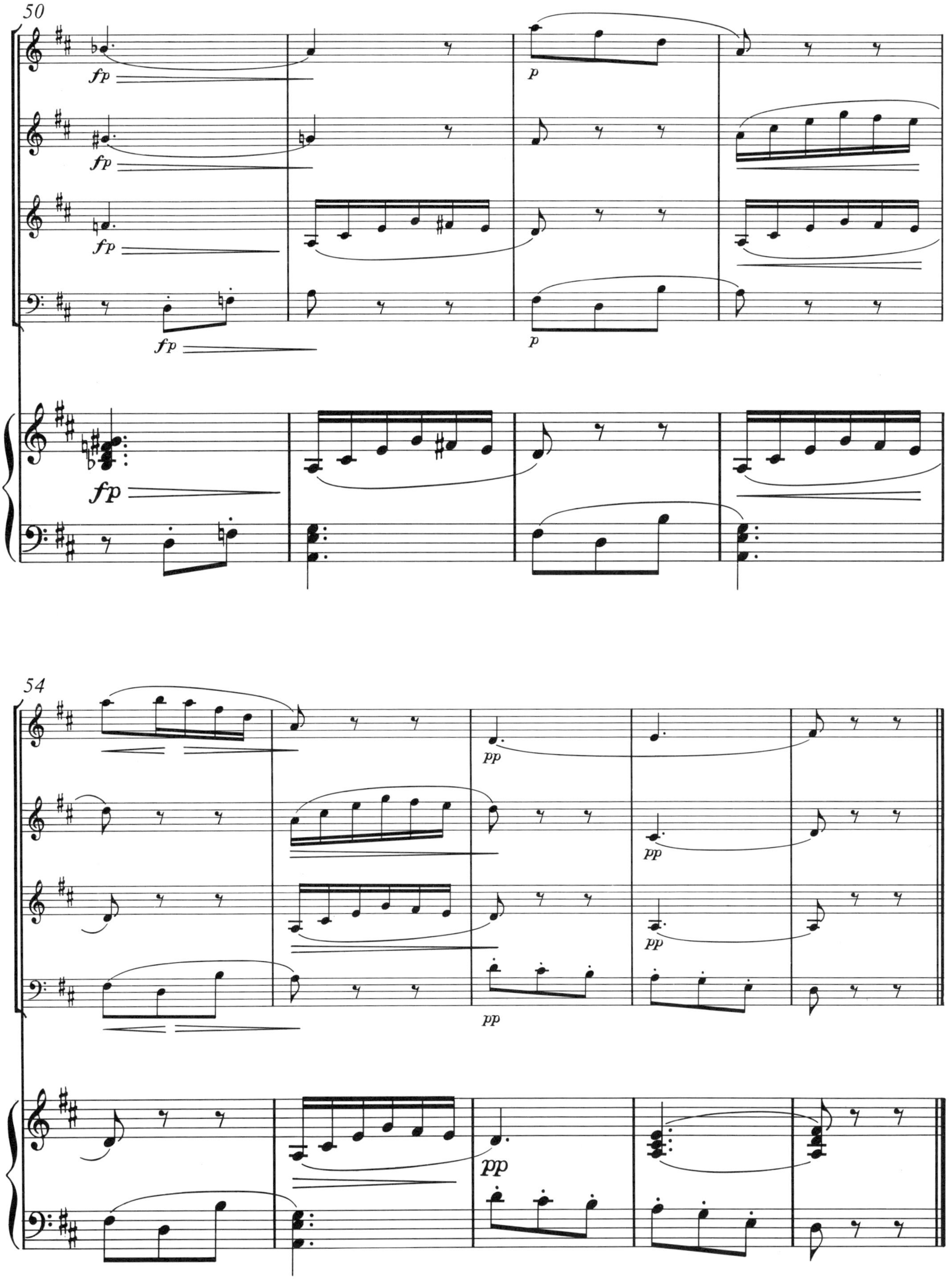
50
fp
fp
fp
fp
fp
p
p
54
pp
pp
pp
pp
pp

Rosamunde
(Overture)

Franz Schubert
(1797-1828)

Nutcracker Suite Op. 71a
(Valse des fleurs)

Peter Ilyich Tchaikovsky
(1840-93)

Symphony No. 41 in C (K 551)

(Trio)

Wolfgang Amadeus Mozart
(1756-91)

Violin Concerto in E minor Op. 64
(Third movement)

Felix Mendelssohn-Bartholdy
(1809-47)

24

Reproduced and printed by Halstan & Co. Ltd., Amersham, Bucks., England